MALAYSIA BORNEO
TRAVEL GUIDE 2025

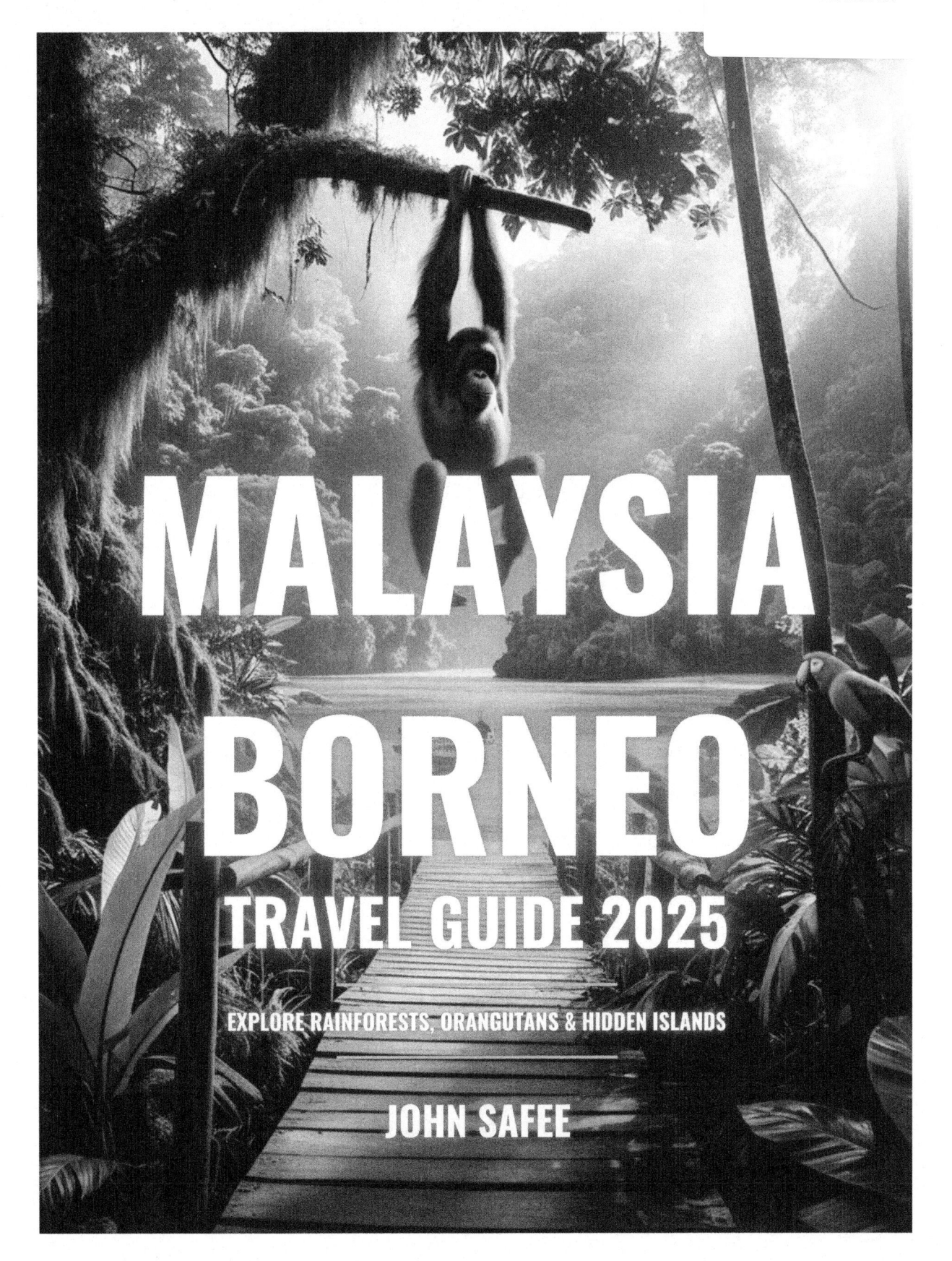

EXPLORE RAINFORESTS, ORANGUTANS & HIDDEN ISLANDS

JOHN SAFEE

Copyright © 2025 by John Safee

All rights reserved. No part of this publication may be reproduced, distributed, or transmitted in any form or by any means, including photocopying, recording, or other electronic or mechanical methods, without the prior written permission of the author, except in the case of brief quotations embodied in critical reviews and certain other noncommercial uses permitted by copyright law.

Disclaimer:

The information provided in this eBook is for general informational purposes only. While every effort has been made to ensure the accuracy and completeness of the information contained herein, the author and publisher assume no responsibility for errors, omissions, or contrary interpretation of the subject matter herein. This eBook does not constitute legal, financial, or travel advice. Readers should consult relevant professionals or experts for specific advice suited to their needs. The author is not liable for any damages arising from the use or misuse of the information contained in this publication.

About the Author

John Safee is a seasoned travel writer, explorer, and eco-tourism advocate with over a decade of experience uncovering the world's most fascinating destinations. With a deep passion for sustainable travel and wildlife conservation, John has ventured across Southeast Asia, documenting hidden paradises and cultural wonders. His work has been featured in top travel publications, and he continues to inspire readers with immersive, in-depth travel guides. Whether trekking through Borneo's rainforests or diving in Sipadan's world-class reefs, John's expertise brings every destination to life.

Table of Contents

Copyright © 2025 by John Safee   2

Disclaimer: 2

About the Author   3

Table of Contents   4

Introduction to Malaysia Borneo   5

   Why Visit Malaysia Borneo in 2025?   5

   Quick Facts & Overview   5

   What Makes Malaysia Borneo Unique?   6

      1. One of the World's Last Great Rainforests   6

      2. A Wildlife Haven Like No Other   6

      3. Diverse Indigenous Cultures and Traditions   6

      4. Spectacular Natural Wonders   7

      5. Adventure Opportunities for Every Type of Traveler   7

   Best Time to Visit   7

   Sustainable and Responsible Travel   8

Chapter 1:   9

   Planning Your Trip   9

      Visas and Entry Requirements   9

         Key Entry Requirements: 9

         Arrival in Malaysia Borneo   9

      Budgeting and Costs   10

- Estimated Daily Budget: 10
- Typical Costs: 10
- Best Time to Visit 11
- Getting There: Flights and Entry Points 11
- Health and Safety 12
  - Vaccinations and Health Precautions 12
  - Travel Insurance 12
  - Emergency Contacts 13
- Cultural Etiquette and Local Customs 13
  - General Etiquette: 13
  - Indigenous Traditions: 13
- Tips for a Smooth Journey 14

Chapter 2: 15

- Getting Around Malaysia Borneo 15
  - Understanding Malaysia Borneo's Geography 15
  - Flights: The Fastest Way to Travel 15
    - Domestic Flights 15
    - Flight Booking Tips 16
  - Buses: Affordable and Reliable for Overland Travel 16
    - Major Bus Routes 16
    - Best Bus Companies 17
    - Bus Travel Tips 17
  - Car Rentals: Freedom to Explore at Your Own Pace 17
    - Pros of Renting a Car 17
    - Things to Consider Before Renting 18

Recommended Car Rental Companies:	18
Taxis and Ride-Hailing Services	18
Tips for Using Ride-Hailing Services	18
Boats and Ferries: Essential for Island Hopping	19
Popular Ferry & Boat Routes	19
Booking Tips:	19
Trains: A Unique Way to Experience Rural Borneo	19
Train Routes	20
Train Travel Tips:	20
Cycling and Walking: Exploring at a Slower Pace	20
Best Places for Cycling:	20
Cycling Rentals & Tours:	20
Travel Tips for Getting Around Malaysia Borneo	21

Chapter 3:   22

Top Destinations in Sabah	22
Kota Kinabalu: The Gateway to Adventure	22
Kinabalu National Park & Mount Kinabalu	23
Sepilok Orangutan Rehabilitation Centre & Rainforest Discovery Centre	23
Sandakan & Turtle Islands Park	24
Kinabatangan River: Wildlife Paradise	24
Danum Valley & Tabin Wildlife Reserve	25
Sipadan Island: World-Class Diving	25

Chapter 4:   27

Top Destinations in Sarawak	27
Kuching: The Cultural Capital of Sarawak	27

    Highlights: ... 27

  Bako National Park: A Wildlife Haven ... 28

    Highlights: ... 28

  Gunung Mulu National Park: A UNESCO World Heritage Site ... 28

    Highlights: ... 29

  Semenggoh Wildlife Centre: Orangutan Encounters ... 29

    Highlights: ... 29

  Sarawak Cultural Village: A Living Museum ... 30

    Highlights: ... 30

  Niah National Park: Prehistoric Caves and Archaeological Wonders ... 30

    Highlights: ... 30

  Iban Longhouse Experience: Immersing in Indigenous Culture ... 31

    Highlights: ... 31

Chapter 5: ... 32

  Wildlife & Nature Experiences in Malaysia Borneo ... 32

    Iconic Wildlife of Borneo ... 32

      Orangutans ... 32

      Bornean Pygmy Elephant ... 33

      Proboscis Monkey ... 33

      Sun Bears ... 33

      Other Notable Species ... 34

    Best Places for Jungle Treks & Rainforest Exploration ... 34

      Danum Valley Conservation Area (Sabah) ... 34

      Mulu National Park (Sarawak) ... 34

      Kinabatangan River (Sabah) ... 35

      Bako National Park (Sarawak) — 35

  Marine & Coastal Wildlife Experiences — 35

      Sipadan Island (Sabah) — 35

      Turtle Islands Park (Sabah) — 36

      Miri-Sibuti Coral Reefs (Sarawak) — 36

  Responsible Wildlife Tourism & Conservation Efforts — 36

Chapter 6: — 38

  Adventure & Outdoor Activities in Malaysia Borneo — 38

    Hiking & Mountain Climbing — 38

      Mount Kinabalu: Conquering Southeast Asia's Tallest Peak — 38

      Mulu Pinnacles: A Challenging Limestone Trek — 38

      Bako National Park: Coastal Trails & Wildlife Encounters — 39

    Scuba Diving & Snorkeling — 39

      Sipadan Island: A World-Class Dive Destination — 39

      Mabul & Kapalai: Macro Diving Paradise — 39

      Tunku Abdul Rahman Marine Park: Accessible Island Adventures — 40

    Wildlife & River Safaris — 40

      Kinabatangan River: Borneo's Wildlife Highway — 40

      Danum Valley: A Remote Rainforest Expedition — 40

    Caving & Spelunking — 41

      Mulu Caves: Exploring the World's Largest Cave Chambers — 41

      Gomantong Caves: A Swarm of Life — 41

    Kayaking & White-Water Rafting — 41

      Padas River: Thrilling White-Water Rafting — 41

      Semadang River: Scenic Kayaking & Wildlife Viewing — 42

Jungle Trekking & Survival Experiences	42
Long Pasia: A Deep Jungle Expedition	42
Batang Ai National Park: Trekking with the Iban Tribe	42
Tips for Adventure Travelers	42

Chapter 7:   44

Cultural & Indigenous Experiences in Malaysia Borneo	44
Meeting the Indigenous Tribes of Borneo	44
Traditional Festivals & Celebrations	46
Cultural Immersion Experiences	46
Local Handicrafts & Souvenirs	47
Responsible Cultural Tourism	48

Chapter 8:   49

Food & Culinary Journey	49
Must-Try Bornean Dishes	49
1. Sarawak Laksa – The State's Signature Dish	49
2. Ambuyat – A Sticky and Unique Delight	50
3. Hinava – Borneo's Answer to Ceviche	50
4. Manok Pansoh – Bamboo Chicken from the Iban Community	51
5. Tuaran Mee – Sabah's Beloved Noodle Dish	51
Best Street Food Spots & Local Markets	52
1. Top Spot Food Court (Kuching, Sarawak)	52
2. Gaya Street Sunday Market (Kota Kinabalu, Sabah)	52
3. Siniawan Night Market (Sarawak)	52
Unique Dining Experiences	52
Jungle Dining in Danum Valley	52

  Iban Longhouse Feasts   52

  Seafood Feasts by the Waterfront   53

 Practical Tips for Exploring Borneo's Food Scene   53

Chapter 9:   54

 Eco-Tourism & Responsible Travel in Malaysia Borneo   54

  Embracing Sustainable Travel in Borneo   54

  Understanding Eco-Tourism in Borneo   54

  Best Practices for Responsible Travelers   54

   1. Choose Eco-Friendly Accommodations   55

   2. Respect Wildlife and Their Natural Habitats   55

   3. Support Local Communities and Indigenous Cultures   55

   4. Minimize Your Environmental Footprint   55

   5. Choose Ethical Tour Operators   56

  Top Eco-Tourism Experiences in Malaysia Borneo   56

   1. Rainforest Trekking and Wildlife Watching   56

   2. River Cruises Along the Kinabatangan River   56

   3. Marine Conservation and Responsible Diving   57

   4. Visiting Indigenous Villages and Learning from Local Communities   57

Chapter 10:   58

 Practical Travel Tips   58

  Understanding Local Customs and Etiquette   58

  Health and Safety Considerations   59

  Money and Budgeting   60

  Transportation and Getting Around   60

  Language and Communication   61

Packing Essentials 61

Sustainable and Responsible Travel 62

Tips for a Smooth Journey 62

Chapter 11: 64

Recommended Itineraries 64

7-Day Adventure Itinerary: Jungles, Wildlife & Mountains 64

Day 1: Arrival in Kota Kinabalu & Island Hopping 64

Day 2: Climb Mount Kinabalu (Day 1) 64

Day 3: Summit Mount Kinabalu & Return 65

Day 4: Sandakan & Sepilok Orangutan Rehabilitation Centre 65

Day 5: Kinabatangan River Safari 65

Day 6: Danum Valley Rainforest Adventure 65

Day 7: Return to Kota Kinabalu & Departure 65

10-Day Culture & Nature Journey 66

Day 1-2: Kota Kinabalu & Mari Mari Cultural Village 66

Day 3-4: Mount Kinabalu & Poring Hot Springs 66

Day 5-6: Sandakan, Sepilok & Kinabatangan River 66

Day 7-8: Kuching & Bako National Park 66

Day 9: Semenggoh Wildlife Centre & Longhouse Stay 66

Day 10: Return to Kuching & Departure 67

14-Day Ultimate Borneo Experience 67

Day 1-2: Kota Kinabalu & Tunku Abdul Rahman Marine Park 67

Day 3-4: Mount Kinabalu & Poring Hot Springs 67

Day 5-6: Sandakan, Sepilok & Kinabatangan River 67

Day 7-8: Danum Valley Conservation Area 67

Day 9-10: Kuching & Bako National Park	67
Day 11-12: Mulu Caves & Pinnacles	68
Day 13-14: Iban Longhouse Experience & Departure	68
Final Thoughts & Resources	**69**
A Place Worth Returning To	69
Supporting Sustainable Tourism	70
Helpful Travel Resources	70
Government & Official Tourism Websites	71
Conservation & Wildlife Organizations	71
Travel Apps & Online Tools	71
Recommended Books & Documentaries	72
Books	72
Documentaries	72
Your Next Destination Awaits	72

Introduction to Malaysia Borneo

Why Visit Malaysia Borneo in 2025?

Malaysia Borneo is one of the world's most extraordinary travel destinations, where lush rainforests meet pristine coastlines, and wildlife thrives in one of the planet's oldest ecosystems. Split between the states of Sabah and Sarawak, Malaysia's portion of Borneo is home to diverse indigenous cultures, breathtaking natural landscapes, and unparalleled adventure opportunities. Whether you're an eco-traveler, a history enthusiast, or a thrill-seeker, Malaysia Borneo offers a travel experience unlike any other.

As 2025 unfolds, Malaysia Borneo continues to evolve as a premier destination for responsible tourism. New conservation efforts, eco-friendly lodges, and improved infrastructure make it easier than ever for travelers to explore its wonders while minimizing their environmental impact. From the misty peaks of Mount Kinabalu to the labyrinthine caves of Mulu, from orangutan sanctuaries to vibrant street markets, Malaysia Borneo is a place where adventure meets authenticity.

Quick Facts & Overview

- **Location:** Southeast Asia, part of the island of Borneo, shared with Indonesia (Kalimantan) and Brunei.
- **Major Cities:** Kota Kinabalu (Sabah), Kuching (Sarawak), Sandakan, Miri, Sibu.
- **Languages:** Malay (official), English (widely spoken), indigenous languages (Iban, Kadazan-Dusun, Bidayuh).
- **Currency:** Malaysian Ringgit (MYR).
- **Time Zone:** Malaysia Standard Time (UTC +8).

- **Climate:** Equatorial rainforest climate with high humidity and warm temperatures year-round.
- **Best Known For:** Rainforests, wildlife (orangutans, pygmy elephants, proboscis monkeys), world-class diving (Sipadan), indigenous cultures, adventure tourism.

What Makes Malaysia Borneo Unique?

1. One of the World's Last Great Rainforests

Malaysia Borneo is home to some of the most ancient and biodiverse rainforests on Earth, with certain areas estimated to be over 140 million years old. These forests shelter thousands of plant and animal species found nowhere else in the world. Danum Valley, Maliau Basin, and the Kinabatangan River provide some of the best opportunities to witness this rich biodiversity up close.

2. A Wildlife Haven Like No Other

Few places on Earth offer such a high concentration of iconic and rare wildlife. Malaysia Borneo is famous for its orangutans, pygmy elephants, and proboscis monkeys, but it's also home to sun bears, clouded leopards, and countless bird species. Conservation centers such as Sepilok Orangutan Rehabilitation Centre and Bornean Sun Bear Conservation Centre allow visitors to learn about ongoing efforts to protect these incredible creatures.

3. Diverse Indigenous Cultures and Traditions

Malaysia Borneo's indigenous communities have inhabited the land for centuries, preserving traditions that remain vibrant today. The Iban, Kadazan-Dusun, Bidayuh, and other ethnic groups offer visitors the opportunity to experience longhouse stays, cultural performances, and traditional festivals such as Gawai and Kaamatan. These experiences provide a deeper connection to the island's history and its people.

4. Spectacular Natural Wonders

Beyond the rainforests, Malaysia Borneo boasts stunning natural landscapes, including the towering granite peak of Mount Kinabalu, the otherworldly limestone formations of Mulu Caves, and the serene beaches of the Tunku Abdul Rahman Marine Park. Each region offers unique geological and ecological wonders that continue to draw adventurers from around the world.

5. Adventure Opportunities for Every Type of Traveler

From trekking through dense jungles to diving in some of the world's best marine ecosystems, Malaysia Borneo caters to every kind of traveler. Whether you're climbing Mount Kinabalu, exploring vast cave systems, rafting down wild rivers, or simply relaxing on a secluded beach, the island's landscapes provide endless opportunities for adventure and discovery.

Best Time to Visit

Malaysia Borneo's tropical climate makes it a year-round destination, but understanding seasonal variations can help you plan the best possible trip.

- **Dry Season (March to October):** Ideal for outdoor activities such as hiking, diving, and wildlife spotting. The driest months are typically May to August.
- **Rainy Season (November to February):** While rains are more frequent, they are usually short-lived. This is a great time to visit waterfalls, witness lush greenery, and enjoy fewer crowds.

- **Wildlife Watching:** Orangutans and other wildlife are more active during fruiting seasons, typically between March and May.
- **Diving Conditions:** Visibility is at its best between April and September, making it the prime time to explore Borneo's underwater treasures.

Sustainable and Responsible Travel

With growing tourism, it is essential to travel responsibly in Malaysia Borneo to protect its fragile ecosystems and support local communities. Choosing eco-friendly accommodations, respecting wildlife, reducing plastic waste, and engaging in ethical tourism practices can ensure that Borneo remains a paradise for future generations.

- **Respect Local Communities:** Engage with indigenous cultures respectfully, support local artisans, and learn about their traditions.
- **Choose Responsible Wildlife Tourism:** Visit ethical wildlife sanctuaries and avoid attractions that exploit animals.
- **Reduce Your Environmental Footprint:** Bring reusable items, avoid single-use plastics, and follow Leave No Trace principles when exploring nature.

Chapter 1:

Planning Your Trip

Planning a trip to Malaysia Borneo is an exciting endeavor, offering the promise of untamed rainforests, extraordinary wildlife, and rich cultural experiences. Whether you're an adventure seeker, a nature enthusiast, or a cultural explorer, careful preparation ensures a smooth and memorable journey. This chapter provides everything you need to know, from entry requirements and budgeting to health precautions and local customs.

Visas and Entry Requirements

Malaysia has relatively relaxed entry requirements, making it accessible for most travelers. Citizens of the United States, Canada, the United Kingdom, Australia, and many European countries can enter Malaysia visa-free for up to 90 days. However, this may vary depending on your nationality, so it's essential to check with the Malaysian Immigration Department before traveling.

Key Entry Requirements:

- A passport valid for at least six months beyond your arrival date
- Proof of onward or return travel
- Sufficient funds to cover your stay
- A visa (if required for your nationality)

For travelers needing a visa, the Malaysian eVisa system offers a convenient online application process. Processing times typically range from a few days to two weeks.

Arrival in Malaysia Borneo

Malaysia Borneo consists of two states, Sabah and Sarawak, each with its own immigration controls. Even if you are traveling domestically from Peninsular Malaysia, you will need to go through passport control when entering Sabah or Sarawak. Keep this in mind when booking flights and allow extra time for immigration checks.

Budgeting and Costs

Malaysia Borneo caters to a wide range of budgets, from backpackers to luxury travelers. Understanding costs will help you plan accordingly and make the most of your trip.

Estimated Daily Budget:

- **Budget Travelers ($30–$50 per day)**: Hostels, public transport, local eateries, and free or low-cost activities such as hiking and national park visits.
- **Mid-Range Travelers ($50–$150 per day)**: Boutique hotels, private transport, guided tours, and occasional fine dining.
- **Luxury Travelers ($150+ per day)**: High-end resorts, private drivers, premium tours, and exclusive wildlife experiences.

Typical Costs:

- Accommodation: Hostel dorms start at $10, budget hotels at $30, and luxury resorts at $150+.
- Food: A meal at a local eatery costs around $3–$5, while a restaurant meal averages $10–$20.
- Transport: Bus fares range from $2–$10, while taxis and private drivers cost more.
- Activities: Entrance to national parks starts at $5, with guided tours costing $50–$150 depending on the experience.

While Malaysia Borneo is generally affordable, certain activities—such as diving in Sipadan or jungle trekking in Danum Valley—can be pricey. Planning ahead allows you to allocate funds to experiences that matter most.

Best Time to Visit

Malaysia Borneo has a tropical climate with warm temperatures year-round. However, the weather can vary depending on the region and season.

- **Dry Season (March–September)**: The best time for outdoor adventures, wildlife spotting, and diving. Fewer rain showers make hiking and jungle trekking more enjoyable.
- **Wet Season (October–February)**: Heavy rains are common, but this is still a great time to visit if you don't mind occasional downpours. The rainforest is lush, waterfalls are at their peak, and fewer tourists mean quieter travel experiences.

Wildlife sightings can occur year-round, but some species, like turtles and migratory birds, have specific seasons. Researching ahead ensures you visit during the best time for your desired activities.

Getting There: Flights and Entry Points

Most travelers arrive in Malaysia Borneo by air, with the two main international airports located in:

- **Kota Kinabalu International Airport (BKI)** – The main gateway to Sabah, with international flights from Singapore, South Korea, Hong Kong, and major Malaysian cities.

- **Kuching International Airport (KCH)** – The primary entry point to Sarawak, serving flights from Kuala Lumpur, Singapore, and Indonesia.

Other airports, such as Sandakan (SDK) and Miri (MYY), handle domestic and regional flights, making it easy to travel within Borneo.

Health and Safety

Malaysia Borneo is a safe destination, but taking a few precautions ensures a trouble-free journey.

Vaccinations and Health Precautions

Before traveling, consult your doctor about recommended vaccinations. The following are commonly advised:

- Hepatitis A and B
- Typhoid
- Tetanus and diphtheria
- Rabies (for those spending extended time in rural areas)

Malaria is present in some remote areas, especially deep in the jungle. While urban centers and most national parks are low-risk, consider anti-malarial medication if visiting regions with high mosquito activity. Dengue fever is also a concern, so using insect repellent and wearing long sleeves helps minimize risk.

Travel Insurance

Comprehensive travel insurance is highly recommended. Policies should cover:

- Medical emergencies and evacuation

- Trip cancellations or interruptions
- Lost or stolen belongings
- Adventure activities such as hiking and scuba diving

Emergency Contacts

- Police and Emergency Services: 999
- Tourist Police: +60 88-450222 (Kota Kinabalu)
- Major Hospitals: Queen Elizabeth Hospital (Sabah), Sarawak General Hospital (Kuching)

Cultural Etiquette and Local Customs

Malaysia Borneo is home to diverse cultures, including Malay, Chinese, and indigenous groups such as the Iban and Kadazan-Dusun. Respecting local customs enhances your travel experience.

General Etiquette:

- Greet people with a smile and a slight nod.
- Use your right hand for giving and receiving items.
- Dress modestly when visiting villages or religious sites.

Indigenous Traditions:

- If invited to a longhouse, remove your shoes before entering.
- Accepting food and drinks from hosts is a sign of respect.
- Avoid pointing at people or objects with your finger—use your thumb instead.

Understanding these customs helps create meaningful interactions and ensures a respectful visit.

Tips for a Smooth Journey

- **Book flights and accommodations in advance**, especially during peak travel months.
- **Pack appropriately for Borneo's climate**, including lightweight clothing, rain gear, and sturdy footwear.
- **Carry cash**, as some remote areas have limited access to ATMs or card payments.
- **Learn a few basic Malay phrases** to connect with locals and navigate easily.

Chapter 2:

Getting Around Malaysia Borneo

Navigating Malaysia Borneo is an adventure in itself. Whether you're traveling through the bustling cities, exploring the dense jungles, or hopping between islands, knowing the best transportation options can enhance your experience. This chapter provides an in-depth look at how to get around efficiently, affordably, and safely.

Understanding Malaysia Borneo's Geography

Malaysia Borneo consists of two states: **Sabah** in the north and **Sarawak** in the south. These states are separated by vast rainforests, mountain ranges, and remote islands, making travel between them unique and often requiring multiple transport modes. While some areas have well-developed infrastructure, others require more adventurous travel arrangements, such as riverboats or chartered flights.

Flights: The Fastest Way to Travel

Due to Borneo's large land area and rugged terrain, flying is often the most efficient way to cover long distances.

Domestic Flights

Several airlines operate domestic flights between major cities and remote areas, making air travel the best option for travelers short on time. Key airports include:

- **Kota Kinabalu International Airport (BKI)** – The main gateway to Sabah.
- **Kuching International Airport (KCH)** – The primary airport for Sarawak.
- **Sandakan Airport (SDK)** – A major hub for travelers heading to Sepilok and the Kinabatangan River.
- **Mulu Airport (MZV)** – The access point for Gunung Mulu National Park.
- **Tawau Airport (TWU)** – The nearest airport for those heading to Sipadan Island for diving.

Best Airlines for Domestic Travel:

- **Malaysia Airlines** – Offers full-service flights with checked baggage and meals.
- **AirAsia** – Budget-friendly, with frequent promotions for cheap fares.
- **MASwings** – A regional airline specializing in flights to remote areas, including the interior of Sarawak and Sabah.

Flight Booking Tips

- Book early to get the best rates, especially for popular routes like Kota Kinabalu to Sandakan.
- Pack light if flying with budget airlines, as they charge extra for checked baggage.
- Check baggage allowances when flying to remote destinations with MASwings, as smaller planes have stricter limits.

Buses: Affordable and Reliable for Overland Travel

Long-distance buses are a budget-friendly way to travel between cities and towns, offering a comfortable journey with air-conditioned coaches.

Major Bus Routes

- **Kota Kinabalu to Sandakan** (6–7 hours) – A scenic drive through mountains and rainforest.
- **Kota Kinabalu to Tawau** (8–9 hours) – Connects to diving hotspots like Sipadan and Mabul Island.
- **Kuching to Miri** (12–14 hours) – A lengthy but affordable alternative to flying.
- **Miri to Limbang** (3–4 hours) – A useful route for those crossing into Brunei.

Best Bus Companies

- **Borneo Express** – Comfortable, well-maintained buses serving major routes in Sabah.
- **Sipitang Express** – A reliable option for travel between Sabah, Sarawak, and Brunei.
- **Biaramas Express** – Covers most of Sarawak's major destinations.

Bus Travel Tips

- Book tickets online or at bus terminals to secure a seat, especially during peak travel seasons.
- Bring snacks and water, as long-distance buses make limited stops.
- Be mindful of delays, especially during the rainy season when road conditions can slow travel.

Car Rentals: Freedom to Explore at Your Own Pace

Renting a car offers flexibility, allowing travelers to explore off-the-beaten-path destinations like the Crocker Range, rural villages, and national parks.

Pros of Renting a Car

- Ideal for self-drive adventures to places with limited public transport.

- Convenient for road trips along scenic routes, such as the drive from Kota Kinabalu to Kundasang.
- Allows easy access to remote areas like Danum Valley without relying on tour operators.

Things to Consider Before Renting

- **Driving License**: International visitors need a valid international driving permit (IDP) along with their national license.
- **Road Conditions**: Major highways are well-paved, but rural roads can be rough, especially after heavy rains.
- **Navigation**: Google Maps and Waze work well, but offline maps are useful in remote areas with weak signal coverage.

Recommended Car Rental Companies:

- **Hertz Malaysia** – Reliable service with a variety of vehicle options.
- **Avis Borneo** – Good for longer rentals and offers insurance coverage.
- **Local Agencies** – Found in major cities, often offering better rates than international chains.

Taxis and Ride-Hailing Services

Taxis are available in cities like Kuching and Kota Kinabalu, but they can be expensive due to lack of meters. Always negotiate the fare before getting in.

Ride-hailing apps like Grab are a more convenient and affordable option for short distances. These services are widely available in major cities and are often cheaper than taxis.

Tips for Using Ride-Hailing Services

- Use **GrabPay** to avoid handling cash.
- Check the fare estimate before booking.
- Be aware that availability may be limited in smaller towns.

Boats and Ferries: Essential for Island Hopping

With its stunning coastline and remote islands, Malaysia Borneo relies heavily on boats and ferries for transportation.

Popular Ferry & Boat Routes

- **Kota Kinabalu to Tunku Abdul Rahman Marine Park** – Short speedboat rides from Jesselton Point to island getaways.
- **Semporna to Sipadan, Mabul, and Kapalai Islands** – Daily boats for divers and snorkelers.
- **Sarawak River Cruise** – A scenic way to explore Kuching's riverside landmarks.
- **Labuan to Brunei** – A convenient ferry route connecting Malaysian Borneo to Brunei.

Booking Tips:

- Arrive early, as boats can fill up quickly.
- Always wear a life jacket, especially on speedboats.
- Check ferry schedules in advance, as services can be affected by weather.

Trains: A Unique Way to Experience Rural Borneo

Sabah's **North Borneo Railway** is the only operational train service, offering a nostalgic journey through villages, plantations, and jungles.

Train Routes

- **Kota Kinabalu to Beaufort** (2 hours) – A scenic ride along the Padas River.
- **Beaufort to Tenom** (2–3 hours) – A charming rural experience popular with adventure travelers heading to the Padas River for white-water rafting.

Train Travel Tips:

- Buy tickets at the station, as online booking options are limited.
- Bring snacks and water, as facilities are basic.
- Travel light, as space for luggage is limited.

Cycling and Walking: Exploring at a Slower Pace

For those who prefer a slower, more immersive travel experience, cycling and walking are great options in certain areas.

Best Places for Cycling:

- **Kota Kinabalu Coastal Path** – A scenic route along the waterfront.
- **Bario Highlands (Sarawak)** – Stunning landscapes and quiet roads for cycling.
- **Kuching Heritage Trail** – Best explored on foot to appreciate the city's colonial charm.

Cycling Rentals & Tours:

- Many guesthouses and hostels offer affordable bike rentals.
- Guided cycling tours are available in Kuching and Kota Kinabalu.

Travel Tips for Getting Around Malaysia Borneo

- Plan transport in advance, especially for remote areas with limited options.
- Be flexible, as weather conditions can disrupt schedules.
- Opt for sustainable travel choices, such as shared transport and eco-friendly tours.

Chapter 3:

Top Destinations in Sabah

Sabah, often referred to as the "Land Below the Wind," is a paradise for nature lovers, adventure seekers, and cultural enthusiasts. This northern state of Malaysian Borneo boasts a stunning mix of lush rainforests, towering mountains, pristine islands, and rich indigenous heritage. From trekking up Southeast Asia's highest peak to encountering orangutans in their natural habitat, Sabah offers experiences that cater to all types of travelers. Here are the must-visit destinations in Sabah that should be on every travel itinerary.

Kota Kinabalu: The Gateway to Adventure

Kota Kinabalu (KK) serves as the capital of Sabah and is the primary entry point for most visitors. This coastal city seamlessly blends urban vibrancy with outdoor adventure. Explore its bustling markets, waterfront attractions, and nearby islands while enjoying breathtaking sunsets over the South China Sea.

- **Gaya Street Sunday Market**: A lively market where visitors can browse local handicrafts, fresh produce, and unique souvenirs.
- **Tunku Abdul Rahman Marine Park**: A cluster of five stunning islands (Gaya, Sapi, Manukan, Mamutik, and Sulug) ideal for snorkeling, diving, and island hopping.
- **Signal Hill Observatory Platform**: The best place for a panoramic view of the city skyline and coastline.

- **Sabah State Museum & Heritage Village**: A great introduction to Sabah's history, culture, and indigenous tribes.
- **Waterfront Esplanade & Night Market**: Perfect for savoring fresh seafood and enjoying the city's nightlife.

Kinabalu National Park & Mount Kinabalu

One of Sabah's crown jewels, Kinabalu National Park is a UNESCO World Heritage Site and home to Mount Kinabalu, Southeast Asia's tallest peak at 4,095 meters. This biologically rich park is a must-visit for hikers, nature lovers, and wildlife enthusiasts.

- **Mount Kinabalu Climb**: A challenging yet rewarding two-day trek to the summit, offering breathtaking sunrise views.
- **Poring Hot Springs**: A relaxing spot with natural hot mineral baths, canopy walks, and butterfly gardens.
- **Kundasang War Memorial**: A tribute to fallen Allied soldiers from World War II, set amidst beautiful gardens with a backdrop of the Crocker Range.
- **Botanical Gardens**: A paradise for botany enthusiasts featuring rare orchids, carnivorous plants, and endemic flora.

Sepilok Orangutan Rehabilitation Centre & Rainforest Discovery Centre

Located near Sandakan, the Sepilok Orangutan Rehabilitation Centre is one of the best places in the world to observe orangutans up close. The center rescues and rehabilitates orphaned and injured orangutans before reintroducing them to the wild.

- **Orangutan Feeding Sessions**: Twice daily feedings offer visitors a chance to see these intelligent primates in a semi-natural environment.
- **Rainforest Discovery Centre (RDC)**: A must-visit for birdwatchers and nature lovers, with canopy walks and trails showcasing Sabah's rich biodiversity.
- **Bornean Sun Bear Conservation Centre**: Just next to Sepilok, this sanctuary is dedicated to the world's smallest bear species.

Sandakan & Turtle Islands Park

Sandakan, once the capital of British North Borneo, is steeped in history and serves as the gateway to some of Sabah's top wildlife experiences.

- **Agnes Keith House**: A beautifully restored colonial home showcasing Sandakan's history under British rule.
- **Sandakan Memorial Park**: A solemn yet important site commemorating prisoners of war during World War II.
- **Turtle Islands Park**: Located off the coast of Sandakan, this marine sanctuary protects nesting sites for endangered green and hawksbill turtles.

Kinabatangan River: Wildlife Paradise

The Kinabatangan River is one of the best places in Southeast Asia for spotting rare and exotic wildlife. A river safari here offers the opportunity to see proboscis monkeys, pygmy elephants, and even wild orangutans.

- **Sunrise & Sunset River Cruises**: The best times for wildlife spotting as animals gather along the riverbanks.

- **Oxbow Lake Excursions**: Tranquil boat rides to see birdlife, crocodiles, and other hidden creatures of the wetlands.
- **Homestays with Indigenous Villages**: An opportunity to learn about the culture and traditions of the Orang Sungai people.

Danum Valley & Tabin Wildlife Reserve

For those who crave deep jungle adventures, Danum Valley Conservation Area and Tabin Wildlife Reserve offer some of the best rainforest experiences in Borneo.

- **Danum Valley**: A pristine, untouched rainforest where travelers can trek through ancient jungle trails, visit waterfalls, and stay at world-class eco-lodges.
- **Wildlife Spotting**: Home to orangutans, clouded leopards, hornbills, and a variety of rare creatures.
- **Tabin Wildlife Reserve**: A great alternative to Danum Valley, featuring natural mud volcanoes where animals gather for mineral-rich soil.

Sipadan Island: World-Class Diving

Rated as one of the best dive sites in the world, Sipadan Island is a dream destination for underwater enthusiasts.

- **Barracuda Point & Turtle Cavern**: Renowned dive sites teeming with marine life, including sea turtles, hammerhead sharks, and swirling schools of barracuda.
- **Diving Permits & Restrictions**: Limited daily permits ensure the island's fragile ecosystem remains protected.

- **Mabul & Kapalai Islands**: Nearby islands offering top-notch dive resorts and excellent muck diving opportunities.

Chapter 4:

Top Destinations in Sarawak

Sarawak, the largest state in Malaysia, is a land of ancient rainforests, majestic rivers, diverse wildlife, and vibrant indigenous cultures. It offers an unparalleled blend of adventure, nature, and heritage, making it an essential stop for any traveler exploring Malaysia Borneo. From the bustling streets of Kuching to the remote caves of Mulu, Sarawak promises unforgettable experiences for nature lovers, culture seekers, and adventure enthusiasts alike.

Kuching: The Cultural Capital of Sarawak

Kuching, Sarawak's charming riverside capital, is a perfect introduction to the state's unique blend of history, culture, and modernity. Known as the "Cat City," Kuching is a compact yet vibrant destination where colonial heritage meets contemporary attractions.

Highlights:

- **Sarawak Museum Complex**: One of the oldest and most comprehensive museums in Malaysia, offering deep insights into Borneo's indigenous cultures, wildlife, and history.
- **Kuching Waterfront**: A picturesque promenade along the Sarawak River, perfect for an evening stroll with stunning views of the Astana and Fort Margherita.
- **Semenggoh Wildlife Centre**: A renowned rehabilitation center where visitors can witness semi-wild orangutans in their natural habitat.
- **Main Bazaar & Carpenter Street**: A haven for handicrafts, antiques, and local street food, including the famous Sarawak laksa and kolo mee.

- **Borneo Cultures Museum**: A modern museum offering interactive exhibits on the indigenous heritage of Sarawak.

Bako National Park: A Wildlife Haven

Just a short boat ride from Kuching, Bako National Park is a paradise for nature lovers and hikers. This is Sarawak's oldest national park and one of the best places to see the elusive proboscis monkey in the wild.

Highlights:

- **Diverse Ecosystems**: Featuring mangroves, dipterocarp forests, and coastal cliffs, offering a range of hiking trails.
- **Wildlife Encounters**: Home to proboscis monkeys, bearded pigs, long-tailed macaques, and numerous bird species.
- **Scenic Trails**: Popular hikes include the Telok Pandan Kecil Trail, which leads to a stunning secluded beach.
- **Unique Rock Formations**: The famous sea stack formation is a must-see, best viewed from a boat.

Gunung Mulu National Park: A UNESCO World Heritage Site

Gunung Mulu National Park is a treasure trove of geological wonders, home to some of the world's most spectacular caves and karst formations. It is a dream destination for spelunkers and adventure seekers.

Highlights:

- **Deer Cave & Lang Cave**: Deer Cave is one of the largest cave passages in the world, home to millions of bats that perform an incredible exodus at dusk.
- **Clearwater Cave**: One of the longest caves in the world, featuring an underground river and stunning limestone formations.
- **The Pinnacles**: A challenging trek to a breathtaking limestone pinnacle formation, offering panoramic views of the rainforest.
- **Canopy Walkway**: One of the world's longest tree canopy walks, providing an unforgettable perspective of the jungle.

Semenggoh Wildlife Centre: Orangutan Encounters

Located just outside Kuching, Semenggoh Wildlife Centre is one of the best places in Borneo to observe semi-wild orangutans. This sanctuary focuses on the rehabilitation of orphaned and rescued orangutans.

Highlights:

- **Orangutan Feeding Sessions**: Best visited during morning and afternoon feeding times when the orangutans emerge from the forest.
- **Conservation Efforts**: Learn about the center's efforts in wildlife rehabilitation and rainforest conservation.
- **Nature Trails**: Short jungle walks where visitors might spot other wildlife, including hornbills and macaques.

Sarawak Cultural Village: A Living Museum

Situated at the foot of Mount Santubong, the Sarawak Cultural Village is an award-winning living museum that showcases the traditions and lifestyles of Sarawak's diverse indigenous groups.

Highlights:

- **Traditional Longhouses**: Explore authentic longhouses of the Iban, Bidayuh, Orang Ulu, and other indigenous tribes.
- **Cultural Performances**: Daily dance and music performances featuring traditional instruments like the sape.
- **Handicraft Demonstrations**: Watch artisans at work, crafting intricate beadwork, weaving, and wood carvings.
- **Interactive Experiences**: Try traditional activities such as blowpipe hunting and rice wine tasting.

Niah National Park: Prehistoric Caves and Archaeological Wonders

Niah National Park is a historically significant site where the earliest human remains in Southeast Asia were discovered. The park's massive limestone caves are both an archaeological wonder and a natural spectacle.

Highlights:

- **Niah Caves**: Home to prehistoric cave paintings and artifacts dating back 40,000 years.

- **The Great Cave**: A colossal chamber that was once a human settlement and is still used for swiftlet nest harvesting.
- **The Painted Cave**: Features ancient rock paintings depicting human figures and animals.
- **Jungle Trails**: Walk through lush rainforests teeming with wildlife before reaching the caves.

Iban Longhouse Experience: Immersing in Indigenous Culture

For an authentic cultural experience, a visit to an Iban longhouse offers a rare glimpse into the traditional lifestyle of Sarawak's largest indigenous group. Many longhouses welcome visitors for homestays, allowing travelers to engage with local communities.

Highlights:

- **Traditional Longhouses**: Wooden communal homes where multiple families live under one roof.
- **Iban Hospitality**: Experience the warmth of Iban culture through storytelling, music, and traditional food.
- **Ngajat Dance Performances**: Witness the graceful warrior dance of the Iban people.
- **Tuak Tasting**: Sample homemade rice wine, a staple of Iban celebrations.

Chapter 5:

Wildlife & Nature Experiences in Malaysia Borneo

Malaysia Borneo is one of the most biodiverse places on Earth, home to lush rainforests, rare wildlife, and unique ecosystems that have remained largely untouched for millennia. Whether you're trekking through dense jungle, cruising along meandering rivers, or diving beneath turquoise waters, nature lovers will find an unparalleled array of experiences. This chapter explores the best wildlife encounters and nature adventures across Sabah and Sarawak, offering insights into where and how to witness Borneo's incredible biodiversity responsibly.

Iconic Wildlife of Borneo

Borneo is home to some of the most extraordinary creatures on the planet, many of which are endemic to the island. Here are the key species you should keep an eye out for:

Orangutans

Often regarded as the face of Borneo's conservation efforts, the critically endangered orangutan is one of the most sought-after wildlife sightings. These gentle primates inhabit the dense lowland and montane forests, using their powerful arms to swing effortlessly through the canopy.

- **Where to See Them:**
    - **Sepilok Orangutan Rehabilitation Centre (Sabah):** A renowned sanctuary where rescued orangutans are rehabilitated before being released back into the wild.

- **Semenggoh Wildlife Centre (Sarawak):** A smaller, equally rewarding reserve near Kuching where semi-wild orangutans come to feed.
- **Danum Valley Conservation Area (Sabah):** For a chance to see fully wild orangutans in an untouched rainforest habitat.

Bornean Pygmy Elephant

The world's smallest elephant species, the Bornean pygmy elephant, is a rare sight but a rewarding one for lucky visitors. These gentle giants roam the forests and riverbanks in family groups.

- **Where to See Them:**
    - **Kinabatangan River (Sabah):** River safaris offer a high chance of spotting these elephants along the banks.
    - **Deramakot Forest Reserve (Sabah):** A lesser-known but excellent location for elephant encounters.

Proboscis Monkey

Known for their comically large noses and potbellies, proboscis monkeys are an iconic Bornean species often seen leaping between mangrove trees.

- **Where to See Them:**
    - **Bako National Park (Sarawak):** A prime location for spotting these monkeys in their natural habitat.
    - **Labuk Bay Proboscis Monkey Sanctuary (Sabah):** A safe haven for proboscis monkeys offering up-close viewing.

Sun Bears

The smallest bear species in the world, the Malayan sun bear, is a rare and elusive forest dweller. Their distinctive golden crescent-shaped chest markings make them easily recognizable.

- **Where to See Them:**
  - **Bornean Sun Bear Conservation Centre (Sabah):** Located next to Sepilok, this center rehabilitates rescued sun bears.

Other Notable Species

- **Clouded Leopard:** A secretive predator, best spotted in Danum Valley or Deramakot Forest.
- **Hornbills:** These striking birds are commonly seen in Kinabatangan, Danum Valley, and Bako National Park.
- **Tarsiers and Slow Lorises:** Nocturnal primates that can be found during guided night walks in forest reserves.

Best Places for Jungle Treks & Rainforest Exploration

Danum Valley Conservation Area (Sabah)

A pristine 438 square-kilometer rainforest, Danum Valley is one of the most biodiverse ecosystems in the world. Visitors can embark on guided jungle treks, canopy walks, and night safaris.

- **Wildlife Highlights:** Wild orangutans, clouded leopards, civets, and hornbills.
- **Activities:** Jungle trekking, birdwatching, night walks.

Mulu National Park (Sarawak)

A UNESCO World Heritage Site, Mulu National Park is famous for its vast c towering limestone pinnacles, and dense rainforest.

- **Wildlife Highlights:** Bats, swiftlets, deer, and various primates.
- **Activities:** Cave exploration, canopy walks, trekking to the Pinnacles.

Kinabatangan River (Sabah)

The Kinabatangan River is one of the best places in Asia for wildlife viewing. Morning and evening boat safaris provide close encounters with Borneo's most iconic species.

- **Wildlife Highlights:** Proboscis monkeys, pygmy elephants, orangutans, crocodiles, hornbills.
- **Activities:** River cruises, birdwatching, night safaris.

Bako National Park (Sarawak)

As Sarawak's oldest national park, Bako offers diverse ecosystems ranging from mangroves to dense jungle. It is one of the best places to see proboscis monkeys.

- **Wildlife Highlights:** Proboscis monkeys, bearded pigs, flying lemurs.
- **Activities:** Hiking, beach visits, wildlife spotting.

Marine & Coastal Wildlife Experiences

Sipadan Island (Sabah)

A world-class diving destination, Sipadan is teeming with marine life, including sea turtles, reef sharks, and massive schools of barracuda.

Green and hawksbill turtles, hammerhead sharks, manta

, snorkeling.

...k is a crucial nesting site for endangered sea turtles.

- **Wildlife Highlights:** Green and hawksbill turtles laying eggs.
- **Activities:** Nighttime turtle watching, conservation programs.

Miri-Sibuti Coral Reefs (Sarawak)

A lesser-known but spectacular diving site with vibrant coral gardens and diverse marine species.

- **Wildlife Highlights:** Reef sharks, nudibranchs, giant groupers.
- **Activities:** Scuba diving, snorkeling.

Responsible Wildlife Tourism & Conservation Efforts

As a visitor, it is essential to engage in responsible tourism that supports conservation. Here's how:

- **Choose Ethical Wildlife Encounters:** Visit rehabilitation centers that focus on conservation rather than animal performances.
- **Support Eco-Tourism Initiatives:** Stay at eco-lodges and participate in community-led wildlife tours.
- **Respect Nature:** Follow guidelines, maintain a safe distance from animals, and avoid feeding wildlife.

- **Reduce Your Environmental Impact:** Use reef-safe sunscreen, avoid single-use plastics, and follow Leave No Trace principles.

Chapter 6:

Adventure & Outdoor Activities in Malaysia Borneo

Malaysia Borneo is a haven for adventure seekers, offering an unparalleled mix of untamed wilderness, towering mountains, world-class dive sites, and hidden caves waiting to be explored. Whether you are trekking through dense jungles, scaling the heights of Mount Kinabalu, diving among vibrant coral reefs, or cruising down wildlife-rich rivers, Borneo's natural beauty provides the ultimate playground for adrenaline enthusiasts. This chapter delves into the top outdoor activities in Malaysia Borneo and how to experience them responsibly.

Hiking & Mountain Climbing

Mount Kinabalu: Conquering Southeast Asia's Tallest Peak

Rising 4,095 meters above sea level, Mount Kinabalu is a bucket-list destination for climbers. Located within Kinabalu National Park, this UNESCO World Heritage Site offers breathtaking views, diverse ecosystems, and an unforgettable summit experience. The climb typically takes two days, with an overnight stay at Laban Rata before making the final ascent to Low's Peak for sunrise. Permits are required, and spots fill up quickly, so booking months in advance is essential.

Mulu Pinnacles: A Challenging Limestone Trek

The razor-sharp limestone formations of the Mulu Pinnacles, within Gunung Mulu National Park, offer one of Borneo's most demanding hikes. The three-day trek involves navigating dense jungle, river crossings, and a steep, strenuous climb to reach the viewpoint. The reward is an awe-inspiring panoramic sight of the jagged rock spires piercing through the lush rainforest canopy.

Bako National Park: Coastal Trails & Wildlife Encounters

Bako National Park in Sarawak features a network of well-marked trails, ranging from easy boardwalks to challenging jungle treks. The trails lead to secluded beaches, cliffside viewpoints, and mangrove forests teeming with proboscis monkeys, bearded pigs, and other unique wildlife. The most popular hike, the Lintang Trail, offers a comprehensive experience of Bako's diverse landscapes.

Scuba Diving & Snorkeling

Sipadan Island: A World-Class Dive Destination

Recognized as one of the best dive sites on the planet, Sipadan Island boasts dramatic underwater walls, abundant marine biodiversity, and crystal-clear waters. Encounters with sea turtles, hammerhead sharks, barracudas, and massive schools of jackfish are common. Access is restricted to preserve the ecosystem, so obtaining a permit in advance is necessary.

Mabul & Kapalai: Macro Diving Paradise

For those who enjoy spotting smaller marine creatures, Mabul and Kapalai offer some of the best macro diving in Southeast Asia. These waters are home to rare critters such as flamboyant cuttlefish, blue-ringed octopuses, and nudibranchs. Snorkeling is also excellent, providing opportunities to observe vibrant coral gardens just meters from shore.

Tunku Abdul Rahman Marine Park: Accessible Island Adventures

Located near Kota Kinabalu, this marine park comprises five islands offering excellent snorkeling and diving opportunities. Gaya Island features coral reefs teeming with marine life, while Sapi and Manukan Islands provide pristine beaches and shallow snorkeling areas ideal for beginners.

Wildlife & River Safaris

Kinabatangan River: Borneo's Wildlife Highway

The Kinabatangan River is a prime destination for spotting wildlife, including orangutans, pygmy elephants, crocodiles, and hornbills. River cruises at dawn and dusk provide the best chances for sightings, as animals emerge from the dense forest to drink and feed along the riverbanks. Many eco-lodges offer guided boat tours, ensuring an immersive experience with knowledgeable naturalists.

Danum Valley: A Remote Rainforest Expedition

For a deeper jungle adventure, Danum Valley Conservation Area offers multi-day treks through one of Borneo's last pristine rainforests. Staying at the Borneo Rainforest Lodge provides access to guided night walks, canopy walks, and chances to see wild orangutans, gibbons, and the elusive clouded leopard.

Caving & Spelunking

Mulu Caves: Exploring the World's Largest Cave Chambers

Gunung Mulu National Park is home to some of the most spectacular caves in the world. Deer Cave, with its massive chamber, houses millions of bats that create a mesmerizing exodus at dusk. Clearwater Cave, one of the longest cave systems in Southeast Asia, features an underground river and stunning limestone formations. Adventure caving tours are available for those seeking a more physically demanding experience, including wading through subterranean rivers and squeezing through narrow passages.

Gomantong Caves: A Swarm of Life

Located near Sandakan, Gomantong Caves are famous for their enormous bat and swiftlet populations. The caves are also home to the traditional practice of bird's nest harvesting, a centuries-old trade. The main chamber is accessible via a wooden walkway, but the adventurous can join guided expeditions into deeper sections of the cave system.

Kayaking & White-Water Rafting

Padas River: Thrilling White-Water Rafting

For adrenaline junkies, white-water rafting on the Padas River offers heart-pounding rapids set against a jungle backdrop. With Grade III-IV rapids, this experience is best suited for thrill-seekers looking for a high-energy adventure. The journey begins with a scenic train ride through rural villages before hitting the wild waters.

Semadang River: Scenic Kayaking & Wildlife Viewing

For a more relaxed experience, the Semadang River near Kuching is ideal for kayaking. The route meanders through limestone cliffs, rainforests, and local villages, providing opportunities to spot kingfishers, monkeys, and even freshwater fish farming operations. Some tours include visits to hidden waterfalls and caves along the way.

Jungle Trekking & Survival Experiences

Long Pasia: A Deep Jungle Expedition

For those seeking an off-the-beaten-path adventure, Long Pasia in Sabah offers a truly remote jungle experience. Guided expeditions take travelers deep into primary rainforests, where they learn survival skills, forage for wild food, and discover ancient burial sites and hidden waterfalls.

Batang Ai National Park: Trekking with the Iban Tribe

Trekking in Batang Ai offers a unique cultural experience as travelers venture into the heart of Sarawak's rainforest with the indigenous Iban people. Multi-day treks lead to traditional longhouses, where visitors can participate in traditional hunting techniques, fishing, and storytelling around the fire.

Tips for Adventure Travelers

- **Respect Nature:** Malaysia Borneo is home to delicate ecosystems. Always follow Leave No Trace principles, avoid single-use plastics, and choose eco-friendly operators.

- **Stay Safe:** Many activities require physical fitness, and some remote locations lack immediate medical access. Travel insurance covering adventure sports is highly recommended.
- **Book in Advance:** Limited permits for popular activities like climbing Mount Kinabalu or diving in Sipadan mean early reservations are essential.
- **Travel with a Guide:** Many jungle treks and wildlife experiences are best undertaken with knowledgeable local guides who can enhance the experience and ensure safety.

Chapter 7:

Cultural & Indigenous Experiences in Malaysia Borneo

Malaysia Borneo is a land of extraordinary cultural diversity, home to over 50 indigenous ethnic groups, each with its own language, traditions, and way of life. Travelers seeking authentic cultural experiences will find a deep connection with the island's rich heritage, from the longhouses of Sarawak to the spiritual rituals of the Kadazan-Dusun in Sabah. This chapter delves into the unique traditions, festivals, and indigenous encounters that make Malaysia Borneo a cultural treasure trove.

Meeting the Indigenous Tribes of Borneo

Borneo's indigenous communities, collectively known as the Dayak people, include the Iban, Bidayuh, and Orang Ulu in Sarawak, and the Kadazan-Dusun and Murut in Sabah. These groups have preserved their traditions for centuries, and visiting their villages offers a glimpse into their daily lives, ancient customs, and remarkable hospitality.

- **Iban People (Sarawak's Former Head-Hunters)**
  The Iban, once feared as headhunters, are now known for their warm hospitality and vibrant culture. Their traditional longhouses, called *rumah panjai*, are communal dwellings where multiple families live under one roof. A visit to an Iban longhouse typically includes a traditional welcome ceremony, where guests are offered *tuak* (rice wine) and entertained with *ngajat* dance performances. Travelers can witness the intricate art of Iban weaving and tattoos, which carry deep spiritual significance.

- **Bidayuh People (Land Dayaks)**

  The Bidayuh, known as the "Land Dayaks," primarily inhabit western Sarawak. Their villages are famous for their circular baruk houses, which were historically used for communal gatherings and defense. Visitors can participate in traditional cooking classes, learn about bamboo musical instruments, and hear legends passed down through generations. The hospitality of the Bidayuh people makes a visit to their villages an enriching experience.

- **Orang Ulu (Upriver People) & Their Unique Art Forms**

  The Orang Ulu communities, including the Kayan, Kenyah, and Penan, are known for their elaborate beadwork, intricate tattooing, and the haunting melodies of the *sape*, a traditional lute-like instrument. Many Orang Ulu villages are located along Sarawak's remote rivers, offering an immersive experience for travelers willing to venture deep into the rainforest.

- **Kadazan-Dusun (The Spiritually Rich Farmers of Sabah)**

  The Kadazan-Dusun are the largest indigenous group in Sabah, known for their agricultural expertise and spiritual traditions. They celebrate the *Kaamatan* harvest festival, a major cultural event featuring rice wine, bamboo dances, and traditional chants known as *sumazau*. Visiting a Kadazan-Dusun village provides insight into their animistic beliefs and the *bobohizan* (spiritual healers) who perform ancient rituals.

- **Murut People (The Last Headhunters of Sabah)**

  The Murut were among the last indigenous groups to abandon headhunting practices. Today, they are celebrated for their blowpipe hunting skills, warrior dances, and *langai* (trampoline-like) bamboo platforms used in traditional celebrations. A visit to a Murut longhouse allows travelers to witness these ancient customs and enjoy their warm hospitality.

Traditional Festivals & Celebrations

Festivals in Borneo are vibrant, community-driven events that offer travelers a firsthand look at indigenous traditions. Planning your trip around these celebrations will allow for a deeper cultural immersion.

- **Gawai Dayak (Sarawak) - June 1-2**
  Gawai Dayak is a grand celebration marking the rice harvest, primarily observed by the Iban and Bidayuh people. The festivities include elaborate feasts, traditional dances, and longhouse gatherings where guests are welcomed with open arms. Expect to witness *tuak*-drinking ceremonies and hear tales of warrior ancestors.
- **Kaamatan (Sabah) - May 30-31**
  Kaamatan, the Kadazan-Dusun harvest festival, is a colorful event featuring *sumazau* dances, beauty pageants (Unduk Ngadau), and a showcase of traditional crafts. This festival provides a fascinating insight into the importance of rice cultivation and the spiritual connection the Kadazan-Dusun have with nature.
- **Rainforest World Music Festival (Sarawak) - July**
  Held annually in the Sarawak Cultural Village near Kuching, this internationally renowned festival brings together indigenous musicians from around the world. It's an excellent opportunity to experience traditional Bornean music, including *sape* performances, while engaging in cultural workshops and craft exhibitions.

Cultural Immersion Experiences

- **Staying in a Traditional Longhouse**
  Spending a night in a longhouse is one of the most immersive cultural experiences in Borneo. Many villages offer homestay programs where guests can join daily activities such as fishing, rice planting, and handicraft making. This experience

provides a rare opportunity to connect with indigenous families and understand their way of life.

- **Learning Traditional Crafts**

  Many indigenous communities have workshops where travelers can learn traditional skills such as basket weaving, beadwork, and wood carving. These crafts are not only beautiful but also hold deep cultural meanings, often passed down through generations.

- **Participating in Rituals & Ceremonies**

  Some villages allow visitors to witness or take part in traditional ceremonies, such as blessing rituals performed by shamans or the preparation of sacred rice wine. These experiences offer a profound understanding of indigenous spirituality and beliefs.

Local Handicrafts & Souvenirs

Authentic handicrafts make for meaningful souvenirs and support local artisans. Some of the best cultural items to bring home include:

- **Pua Kumbu** (Iban woven textiles) – Often used in ceremonies, these intricately designed fabrics are rich in symbolic meaning.
- **Sape** (Orang Ulu musical instrument) – A beautifully carved wooden instrument played in traditional music.
- **Beadwork Jewelry** – Worn by many indigenous groups, these handmade pieces showcase incredible craftsmanship.
- **Blowpipes & Wooden Carvings** – Made by the Penan and Murut people, these items reflect their hunting heritage.

Responsible Cultural Tourism

Engaging with indigenous communities should always be done with respect and sensitivity. Here are some key guidelines:

- **Ask for Permission** – Always seek permission before taking photos, especially of elders and sacred sites.
- **Respect Traditions** – Follow local customs, such as removing shoes before entering a longhouse.
- **Support Local Artisans** – Buy directly from indigenous craftsmen rather than mass-produced souvenirs.
- **Be Mindful of Cultural Appropriation** – Appreciate traditional attire and practices without misrepresenting them.

Chapter 8:

Food & Culinary Journey

Malaysia Borneo is a paradise for food lovers, offering a tantalizing mix of indigenous traditions, Malay, Chinese, and Indian influences, and an abundance of fresh, tropical ingredients. The island's diverse communities—ranging from the Iban and Kadazan-Dusun in Sarawak and Sabah to the Chinese and Malay populations in bustling cities—have created a unique and flavorful cuisine that reflects the region's rich cultural heritage.

From smoky jungle feasts cooked in bamboo to fragrant seafood dishes infused with local spices, every meal tells a story of tradition, community, and the land's natural bounty. This chapter explores the must-try dishes, the best street food spots, unique dining experiences, and practical tips for navigating Borneo's vibrant food scene.

Must-Try Bornean Dishes

1. Sarawak Laksa – The State's Signature Dish

Sarawak Laksa is a dish that embodies the region's multicultural essence. Unlike the fiery, coconut-based laksa found in Peninsular Malaysia, Sarawak Laksa features a delicate, slightly tangy broth made from sambal belacan (fermented shrimp paste), tamarind, and a blend of over twenty spices. The soup is poured over thin rice vermicelli, shredded chicken, fresh prawns, and bean sprouts, topped with a squeeze of calamansi lime and a sprinkle of coriander.

Best enjoyed at:

- **Chong Choon Café (Kuching)** – One of the most famous spots, serving a rich and flavorful version of this classic.
- **Golden Arch Garden Laksa (Kuching)** – Known for its slightly spicier take on Sarawak Laksa.

2. Ambuyat – A Sticky and Unique Delight

A staple among the Bruneian Malay and indigenous communities, Ambuyat is a starchy, glue-like dish made from sago palm starch mixed with boiling water. Traditionally eaten with a two-pronged bamboo stick called a *candasa*, the sticky mass is dipped into a variety of flavorful sauces, including sour *binjai* (wild mango) sauce or fermented shrimp paste. Ambuyat is more about the experience than the taste, offering a window into the island's age-old culinary customs.

Best enjoyed at:

- Local Bruneian Malay eateries in Sabah and Sarawak.
- Restaurants specializing in indigenous cuisine.

3. Hinava – Borneo's Answer to Ceviche

A signature Kadazan-Dusun dish from Sabah, Hinava is a refreshing raw fish salad made with thinly sliced mackerel or tuna marinated in lime juice, shallots, grated ginger, and bird's eye chilies. Sometimes mixed with bitter gourd or wild mango, it's a light yet intensely flavorful dish that perfectly complements the region's tropical climate.

Best enjoyed at:

- **Seri Selera Kampung Air (Kota Kinabalu)** – A seafood haven offering fresh, locally caught fish prepared in traditional styles.

- Kadazan-Dusun cultural villages and homestays.

4. Manok Pansoh – Bamboo Chicken from the Iban Community

Manok Pansoh is a traditional Iban dish where marinated chicken is stuffed into bamboo stalks along with lemongrass, garlic, and tapioca leaves, then slow-cooked over an open fire. The bamboo imparts a unique smoky aroma, and the chicken becomes tender and juicy. This dish is often prepared for celebrations, feasts, and gatherings in longhouses.

Best enjoyed at:

- Iban longhouse stays in Sarawak.
- Cultural restaurants in Kuching.

5. Tuaran Mee – Sabah's Beloved Noodle Dish

Hailing from the town of Tuaran, this egg noodle dish is wok-fried to golden perfection, resulting in a slightly crispy texture. It is usually tossed with pork, egg rolls, and spring onions, with a side of sambal for an extra kick. Some variations include seafood or chicken, making it a versatile and delicious comfort food.

Best enjoyed at:

- **Tuaran Mee Restoran (Tuaran)** – The most authentic version, prepared by local Hakka chefs.
- **Yee Fung Laksa (Kota Kinabalu)** – A famous eatery also known for its laksa.

Best Street Food Spots & Local Markets

1. Top Spot Food Court (Kuching, Sarawak)

Located on a rooftop, this vibrant food court is a seafood lover's paradise. Visitors can choose from fresh catches like crabs, prawns, and clams, which are cooked to order in styles ranging from butter prawns to stir-fried midin (wild jungle ferns).

2. Gaya Street Sunday Market (Kota Kinabalu, Sabah)

A bustling weekend market where you can sample street food like grilled satay, steamed buns, and pandan-flavored desserts. It's also a great place to try traditional Kadazan-Dusun snacks such as *linopot* (rice wrapped in leaf) and banana fritters.

3. Siniawan Night Market (Sarawak)

This charming night market near Kuching offers an old-town atmosphere with wooden shophouses and fairy lights. Highlights include pork satay, deep-fried mushrooms, and Sarawak-style fried kueh tiaw.

Unique Dining Experiences

Jungle Dining in Danum Valley

For an unforgettable experience, head deep into Borneo's rainforests for a candlelit dinner surrounded by nature. Several eco-lodges offer meals using ingredients sourced from the jungle, including wild vegetables and river fish cooked in traditional styles.

Iban Longhouse Feasts

Visiting an Iban longhouse is not just about witnessing their way of life but also indulging in a communal feast featuring bamboo-cooked meats, paku (wild ferns), and tuak (homemade rice wine).

Seafood Feasts by the Waterfront

Sabah is famous for its fresh seafood, and places like Kota Kinabalu's Todak Waterfront Seafood Market allow diners to pick live fish, lobsters, and crabs, which are then cooked to their preference.

Practical Tips for Exploring Borneo's Food Scene

- **Try local markets early in the day.** Many street vendors sell out by mid-morning.
- **Respect cultural eating customs.** For example, in indigenous communities, it's polite to wait for the eldest person to start eating first.
- **Be adventurous, but mindful.** While exotic foods like *butod* (sago worms) are part of Borneo's food culture, always check freshness and hygiene before trying unusual dishes.
- **Ask for recommendations.** Locals are usually eager to share their favorite spots, often leading to hidden culinary gems.
- **Stay hydrated and pace yourself.** With so many flavors to explore, it's best to enjoy meals throughout the day rather than overindulging in one sitting.

Chapter 9:

Eco-Tourism & Responsible Travel in Malaysia Borneo

Embracing Sustainable Travel in Borneo

Malaysia Borneo is a paradise for nature lovers, offering pristine rainforests, unique wildlife, and vibrant indigenous cultures. However, with increased tourism comes the responsibility to protect this fragile ecosystem. Eco-tourism and responsible travel are essential in ensuring that Borneo's natural beauty and cultural heritage are preserved for future generations.

Understanding Eco-Tourism in Borneo

Eco-tourism focuses on minimizing environmental impact while promoting conservation and supporting local communities. This travel approach benefits both visitors and the destination by ensuring sustainable development, ethical wildlife encounters, and meaningful cultural exchanges.

Best Practices for Responsible Travelers

To travel responsibly in Borneo, it is important to adopt sustainable habits that contribute positively to the environment and local communities. Here are key practices every traveler should follow:

1. Choose Eco-Friendly Accommodations

- Stay in eco-lodges or sustainable hotels that prioritize conservation efforts, such as using renewable energy, reducing waste, and supporting local employment.
- Examples include the Sukau Rainforest Lodge (Kinabatangan River) and Borneo Rainforest Lodge (Danum Valley), which actively participate in conservation programs and eco-friendly operations.

2. Respect Wildlife and Their Natural Habitats

- Observe animals from a distance without disturbing their natural behaviors.
- Avoid attractions that promote unethical animal interactions, such as elephant riding or holding orangutans.
- Visit responsible sanctuaries like the Sepilok Orangutan Rehabilitation Centre and Borneo Sun Bear Conservation Centre, which focus on rehabilitation and conservation.

3. Support Local Communities and Indigenous Cultures

- Engage with local communities by staying in traditional longhouses and participating in cultural activities.
- Purchase handmade crafts and products directly from indigenous artisans rather than mass-produced souvenirs.
- Learn about and respect cultural customs, including proper greetings, dress codes, and dining etiquette.

4. Minimize Your Environmental Footprint

- Use reusable water bottles, shopping bags, and utensils to reduce plastic waste.
- Dispose of trash responsibly and participate in eco-cleanup initiatives where possible.

- Choose biodegradable or reef-safe sunscreens to protect marine life when swimming or diving.

5. Choose Ethical Tour Operators

- Opt for tour operators that follow sustainable tourism principles, such as small group tours, wildlife-friendly practices, and low-impact travel.
- Look for operators certified by organizations like Travelife or those partnering with conservation groups.

Top Eco-Tourism Experiences in Malaysia Borneo

Borneo offers a wealth of eco-tourism activities that allow travelers to explore responsibly while contributing to conservation efforts.

1. Rainforest Trekking and Wildlife Watching

- Explore Kinabalu National Park, a UNESCO World Heritage Site, known for its biodiversity and well-maintained trails.
- Trek through Danum Valley, home to endangered species such as pygmy elephants and clouded leopards, and stay at research-based eco-lodges.
- Visit Tabin Wildlife Reserve for an immersive jungle experience, including wildlife spotting and natural mud volcanoes.

2. River Cruises Along the Kinabatangan River

- One of the best ways to see wildlife ethically is by taking a guided river safari along the Kinabatangan River.
- Spot proboscis monkeys, hornbills, and even pygmy elephants while learning about conservation efforts from knowledgeable guides.

3. Marine Conservation and Responsible Diving

- Malaysia Borneo is home to world-renowned diving sites, including Sipadan, Mabul, and Kapalai.
- Choose dive centers that support reef conservation, marine life protection, and sustainable diving practices.
- Participate in marine conservation programs such as reef restoration projects and beach cleanups.

4. Visiting Indigenous Villages and Learning from Local Communities

- Experience the traditional lifestyle of the Iban and Kadazan-Dusun tribes by staying in longhouses and joining cultural ceremonies.
- Learn about sustainable farming practices and traditional crafts while supporting community-based tourism initiatives.

Chapter 10:

Practical Travel Tips

Traveling to Malaysia Borneo is an adventure filled with incredible landscapes, diverse wildlife, and rich cultural heritage. Whether you're trekking through ancient rainforests, diving in pristine waters, or experiencing indigenous traditions, being well-prepared ensures a smooth and enjoyable trip. This chapter provides essential practical travel tips to help you navigate Malaysia Borneo efficiently, stay safe, and make the most of your journey.

Understanding Local Customs and Etiquette

Malaysia Borneo is home to a diverse mix of cultures, including Malay, Chinese, Indian, and numerous indigenous groups such as the Iban, Kadazan-Dusun, and Bidayuh. Respecting local customs is crucial to having a positive experience.

- **Greetings:** A simple handshake or a slight nod is common when meeting locals. The traditional Malay greeting, "Salam," is similar to a handshake but with a touch to the heart.
- **Dress Modestly:** In urban areas, casual clothing is acceptable, but in rural or religious sites, opt for modest attire covering shoulders and knees.
- **Shoes Off:** Remove shoes before entering homes, temples, and some traditional longhouses.
- **Use the Right Hand:** When handing objects, eating, or gesturing, use your right hand, as the left is considered unclean in local customs.

- **Public Displays of Affection:** Keep PDA to a minimum, as conservative communities may find it inappropriate.
- **Respect for Wildlife:** Never feed, touch, or disturb wild animals, especially in conservation areas.

Health and Safety Considerations

Borneo's remote landscapes and tropical climate require travelers to take some health precautions.

- **Vaccinations:** Ensure routine vaccinations are up to date. Recommended vaccines include Hepatitis A and B, typhoid, and tetanus. Consider rabies and Japanese encephalitis if venturing into rural areas.
- **Mosquito Protection:** Malaria and dengue fever are present in some areas. Use insect repellent with DEET, wear long sleeves, and sleep under mosquito nets when necessary.
- **Drinking Water:** Stick to bottled or filtered water. Avoid consuming ice in rural areas where water purification may be uncertain.
- **Medical Kit:** Carry essentials like antiseptic, pain relievers, anti-diarrheal medication, and any personal prescriptions.
- **Emergency Contacts:** Familiarize yourself with emergency numbers: 999 (Police & Ambulance) and 998 (Fire & Rescue).
- **Travel Insurance:** A comprehensive policy covering medical emergencies, evacuations, and adventure activities is essential.

Money and Budgeting

Malaysia Borneo is generally affordable, but costs can vary based on travel style.

- **Currency:** The Malaysian Ringgit (MYR) is the official currency. Cash is essential in rural areas, while credit cards are widely accepted in cities.
- **ATMs and Banks:** Available in major towns but scarce in remote locations. Withdraw enough cash before heading into less-developed regions.
- **Tipping:** Not mandatory but appreciated in restaurants, hotels, and for guides or drivers.
- **Daily Budget Estimates:**
    - Budget travelers: $30–$50 per day
    - Mid-range travelers: $60–$120 per day
    - Luxury travelers: $150+ per day

Transportation and Getting Around

Borneo's vast terrain makes transportation a crucial part of trip planning.

- **Domestic Flights:** The fastest way to travel between Sabah and Sarawak or to remote areas like Mulu and Tawau.
- **Buses and Minivans:** Affordable for intercity travel but may not always be punctual.
- **Car Rentals:** Useful for self-drive explorations but requires an international driving permit.
- **Taxis and Ride-Hailing:** Grab is widely available in urban areas and more affordable than traditional taxis.

- **Boats and Ferries:** Essential for island trips, river cruises, and national park access.
- **Jungle Treks and 4WD Rides:** Necessary for reaching deep rainforest lodges and remote villages.

Language and Communication

While English is widely spoken in tourist areas, learning a few local phrases can enhance your experience.

- **Malay Basics:**
  - Hello – "Halo"
  - Thank you – "Terima kasih"
  - How much? – "Berapa harga?"
  - Where is…? – "Di mana…?"
  - I need help – "Saya perlukan bantuan"
- **Mobile Connectivity:** Local SIM cards (Celcom, Digi, Maxis) offer good coverage. Wi-Fi is common in hotels but may be weak in remote areas.

Packing Essentials

Packing smart ensures comfort and preparedness for Borneo's humid climate and diverse terrain.

- **Clothing:** Lightweight, breathable clothing, rain jacket, and sturdy hiking shoes.
- **Adventure Gear:** Binoculars for wildlife spotting, waterproof bags for boat trips, and headlamps for caves.

- **Electronics:** Universal adapter, power bank, and camera with extra batteries.
- **Documents:** Passport, visa (if required), printed copies of bookings, and travel insurance details.

Sustainable and Responsible Travel

Preserving Borneo's natural and cultural heritage is crucial for future generations.

- **Support Eco-Tourism:** Choose eco-lodges, responsible tour operators, and ethical wildlife experiences.
- **Reduce Plastic Waste:** Bring a reusable water bottle, avoid plastic bags, and say no to straws.
- **Respect Local Communities:** Seek permission before photographing people and support local artisans.
- **Leave No Trace:** Follow national park guidelines, dispose of waste responsibly, and respect wildlife habitats.

Tips for a Smooth Journey

- **Plan for Unpredictability:** Borneo's weather can be unpredictable, so allow flexibility in your itinerary.
- **Book Activities in Advance:** Popular experiences like Mount Kinabalu climbs and Mulu cave tours fill up quickly.
- **Keep Emergency Cash:** Some areas have limited banking services, so always carry extra cash for emergencies.

- **Stay Open-Minded:** Embrace new experiences, interact with locals, and appreciate the diverse cultures and landscapes of Malaysia Borneo.

Chapter 11:

Recommended Itineraries

Borneo is a land of untamed rainforests, rare wildlife, rich indigenous cultures, and stunning coastlines. With so much to explore, planning an itinerary can feel overwhelming. To help streamline your journey, here are three well-crafted itineraries tailored for different travel styles—adventure seekers, cultural enthusiasts, and those looking for a balanced mix of both. Each itinerary ensures a seamless travel experience while maximizing the wonders of Malaysia Borneo.

7-Day Adventure Itinerary: Jungles, Wildlife & Mountains

This itinerary is ideal for thrill-seekers looking to experience the best of Borneo's nature, from trekking to diving and wildlife encounters.

Day 1: Arrival in Kota Kinabalu & Island Hopping

- Arrive in Kota Kinabalu, the gateway to Sabah.
- Explore Tunku Abdul Rahman Marine Park for snorkeling and island hopping.
- Enjoy a seafood dinner at Kota Kinabalu's waterfront.

Day 2: Climb Mount Kinabalu (Day 1)

- Transfer to Kinabalu National Park.
- Begin your ascent of Mount Kinabalu with an overnight stay at Laban Rata Resthouse.

Day 3: Summit Mount Kinabalu & Return

- Reach the summit at sunrise for breathtaking views.
- Descend to the park headquarters and return to Kota Kinabalu.
- Relax at the Poring Hot Springs.

Day 4: Sandakan & Sepilok Orangutan Rehabilitation Centre

- Fly to Sandakan and visit Sepilok Orangutan Rehabilitation Centre.
- Explore the Bornean Sun Bear Conservation Centre.
- Overnight stay in Sepilok or Sandakan.

Day 5: Kinabatangan River Safari

- Travel to the Kinabatangan River for a river safari.
- Spot proboscis monkeys, pygmy elephants, and crocodiles.
- Overnight at an eco-lodge along the river.

Day 6: Danum Valley Rainforest Adventure

- Transfer to Danum Valley for jungle trekking.
- Experience the ancient rainforest and look for wild orangutans and hornbills.
- Stay at a rainforest lodge.

Day 7: Return to Kota Kinabalu & Departure

- Travel back to Kota Kinabalu.
- Enjoy a final meal before departure.

10-Day Culture & Nature Journey

Perfect for those seeking a balance of cultural immersion, wildlife experiences, and scenic beauty across both Sabah and Sarawak.

Day 1-2: Kota Kinabalu & Mari Mari Cultural Village

- Arrive in Kota Kinabalu and explore the city.
- Visit the Mari Mari Cultural Village for an introduction to Sabah's indigenous tribes.
- Explore Kota Kinabalu's markets and waterfront.

Day 3-4: Mount Kinabalu & Poring Hot Springs

- Take a day trek in Kinabalu National Park.
- Visit Poring Hot Springs and Canopy Walkway.

Day 5-6: Sandakan, Sepilok & Kinabatangan River

- Fly to Sandakan and explore Sepilok Orangutan Rehabilitation Centre.
- Experience a Kinabatangan River wildlife cruise.

Day 7-8: Kuching & Bako National Park

- Fly to Kuching in Sarawak.
- Visit the historic city, explore Chinatown, and try Sarawak Laksa.
- Take a day trip to Bako National Park to see proboscis monkeys.

Day 9: Semenggoh Wildlife Centre & Longhouse Stay

- Visit Semenggoh Wildlife Centre for another chance to see orangutans.
- Experience an Iban longhouse stay along the Batang Ai River.

Day 10: Return to Kuching & Departure

- Travel back to Kuching for a final city exploration.
- Depart from Kuching International Airport.

14-Day Ultimate Borneo Experience

For travelers who want to see it all, this two-week itinerary covers the best of Sabah and Sarawak, blending adventure, wildlife, and cultural encounters.

Day 1-2: Kota Kinabalu & Tunku Abdul Rahman Marine Park

- Explore Kota Kinabalu and go island hopping.

Day 3-4: Mount Kinabalu & Poring Hot Springs

- Climb Mount Kinabalu (or hike in Kinabalu National Park).
- Relax at Poring Hot Springs.

Day 5-6: Sandakan, Sepilok & Kinabatangan River

- Fly to Sandakan, visit Sepilok, and take a Kinabatangan River safari.

Day 7-8: Danum Valley Conservation Area

- Trek through Danum Valley's pristine rainforest.

Day 9-10: Kuching & Bako National Park

- Fly to Kuching and visit Bako National Park.

Day 11-12: Mulu Caves & Pinnacles

- Fly to Gunung Mulu National Park.
- Explore Deer Cave, Lang Cave, and the Pinnacles trek.

Day 13-14: Iban Longhouse Experience & Departure

- Visit an Iban longhouse for an immersive cultural experience.
- Return to Kuching and fly home.

Final Thoughts & Resources

Malaysia Borneo is a land of untamed wilderness, vibrant cultures, and breathtaking natural wonders. Whether you've explored its misty rainforests, dived into the turquoise waters of its coral reefs, or immersed yourself in the traditions of its indigenous communities, one thing is certain—Borneo is a destination that leaves a lasting impression.

As your journey comes to an end, you'll find that Borneo is not just a place to visit but an experience that transforms how you see the world. The memories of orangutans swinging through ancient trees, the rhythmic sounds of tribal celebrations, and the taste of freshly caught seafood by the sea will stay with you long after you leave.

A Place Worth Returning To

One of the most beautiful aspects of Borneo is its endless potential for discovery. No matter how many days you've spent trekking its jungles or relaxing on its beaches, there will always be new places to uncover and fresh experiences to enjoy. Conservation efforts continue to open up more opportunities for sustainable tourism, and with each passing year, the island offers more ways for travelers to engage with its natural and cultural heritage responsibly.

Whether you visited as an adventurer, nature enthusiast, or cultural explorer, Borneo's unique charm will likely call you back. Many who visit find themselves planning a return trip, drawn once again by its biodiversity, warm hospitality, and sense of raw adventure.

Supporting Sustainable Tourism

Borneo's natural beauty and rich traditions remain intact largely due to dedicated conservation efforts and responsible tourism practices. As you reflect on your journey, consider how your travel choices can contribute positively to the region's long-term sustainability.

- **Choose Eco-Friendly Accommodations:** Support lodges and resorts that prioritize sustainability, such as solar-powered operations, waste reduction programs, and partnerships with local communities.
- **Respect Wildlife & Nature:** Follow ethical guidelines when observing wildlife. Never feed animals, avoid flash photography near sensitive species, and keep a respectful distance.
- **Engage with Local Communities:** Purchasing locally made crafts, participating in cultural exchanges, and dining at family-owned restaurants help preserve traditions and support the local economy.
- **Minimize Plastic Waste:** Bring a reusable water bottle, say no to single-use plastics, and use biodegradable toiletries to reduce your environmental footprint.

By practicing responsible tourism, you help ensure that Borneo remains a thriving destination for future generations of travelers and locals alike.

Helpful Travel Resources

To make your journey smoother and more informed, here are some trusted resources that can assist you before, during, and after your trip:

Government & Official Tourism Websites

- **Tourism Malaysia** (www.malaysia.travel) – The official tourism board providing updated travel information, events, and guides.
- **Sabah Tourism Board** (www.sabahtourism.com) – A comprehensive resource for travel in Sabah, covering attractions, accommodations, and conservation initiatives.
- **Sarawak Tourism Board** (www.sarawaktourism.com) – The go-to site for cultural and nature-based travel experiences in Sarawak.
- **Immigration Department of Malaysia** (www.imi.gov.my) – Visa requirements, entry policies, and other travel regulations.

Conservation & Wildlife Organizations

- **WWF-Malaysia** (www.wwf.org.my) – Focuses on conservation efforts for Borneo's wildlife, forests, and marine ecosystems.
- **Borneo Orangutan Survival Foundation** (www.orangutan.or.id) – Supports orangutan rehabilitation and conservation programs.
- **Marine Research Foundation** (www.mrf-asia.org) – Dedicated to marine conservation, including turtle protection and coral reef preservation.

Travel Apps & Online Tools

- **Maps.me** – Offline maps that help navigate remote areas where internet access is limited.
- **Google Translate** – Useful for translating Bahasa Malaysia and other local dialects.
- **Grab** – The most reliable ride-hailing app in Malaysia for taxis and private car services.
- **XE Currency Converter** – Real-time exchange rates for managing travel budgets.

- **Malaysia Airlines & AirAsia Apps** – Essential for booking and managing domestic flights.

Recommended Books & Documentaries

For travelers who want to deepen their understanding of Borneo's history, wildlife, and cultures, these books and documentaries provide valuable insights:

Books

- *Into the Heart of Borneo* by Redmond O'Hanlon – A classic travelogue detailing an adventurous journey through Borneo's interior.
- *The Last Wild Men of Borneo* by Carl Hoffman – A fascinating look at the lives of two men drawn to Borneo's untamed wilderness.
- *Wild Borneo: The Wildlife and Scenery of Sabah, Sarawak, Brunei, and Kalimantan* by Nick Garbutt and Cede Prudente – A visually stunning guide to Borneo's diverse ecosystems.

Documentaries

- *Borneo: Earth's Ancient Isle* (BBC) – A breathtaking look at Borneo's wildlife and rainforests.
- *Orangutan Jungle School* (Love Nature) – Follows the journey of rescued orangutans as they prepare for life in the wild.
- *Lost Worlds of Borneo* (National Geographic) – Explores hidden caves, ancient rainforests, and the incredible biodiversity of the island.

Your Next Destination Awaits

As you conclude your Borneo adventure, you might already be thinking about your next great journey. Whether it's exploring more of Malaysia's mainland, venturing to another

Southeast Asian gem, or embarking on a new kind of adventure entirely, travel is a never-ending opportunity for discovery.

If Borneo has inspired you to seek out nature, connect with different cultures, and travel more sustainably, then this journey has been more than just a trip—it's been a step toward a deeper appreciation of the world around you.

Wherever you go next, may your travels be filled with adventure, learning, and unforgettable experiences. Safe travels, and see you on the road again.

Printed in Dunstable, United Kingdom